It's great fun decorating the tree! See if you can find ten stars in the picture, then colour it in.

Look at Santa soaring above the rooftops!
Colour him and his magical team of reindeer.

Santa is on his way! Colour him in
with your very best colouring.

Colour in this busy elf while he does his job in Santa's workshop.

What comes next? Look at the picture patterns going down the page, and fill in the blanks.

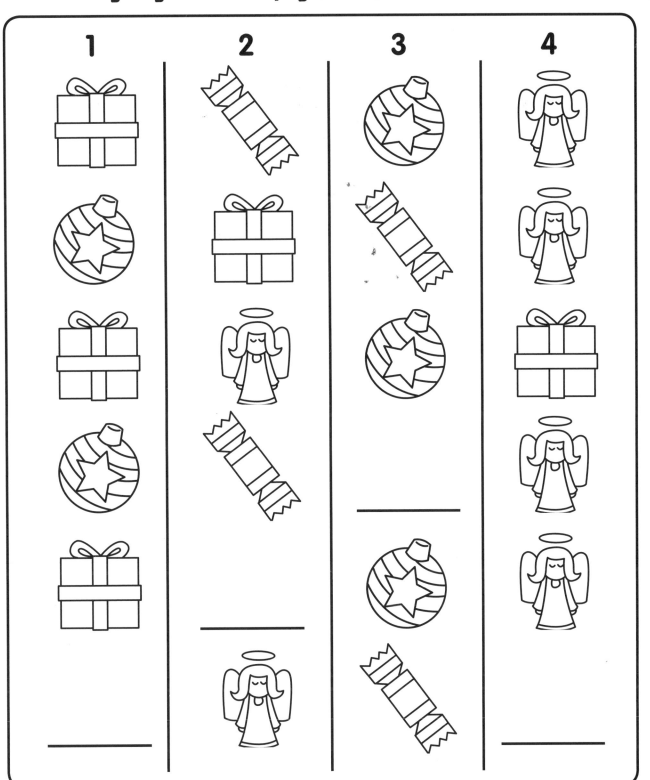

Lottie is fast asleep on Christmas Eve. See if you can spot eight differences between the two pictures.

Make your own snowman by adding clothes and a face to this picture.

Jingle bells, jingle bells, jingle all the way!
Sing along as you colour these jolly bells.

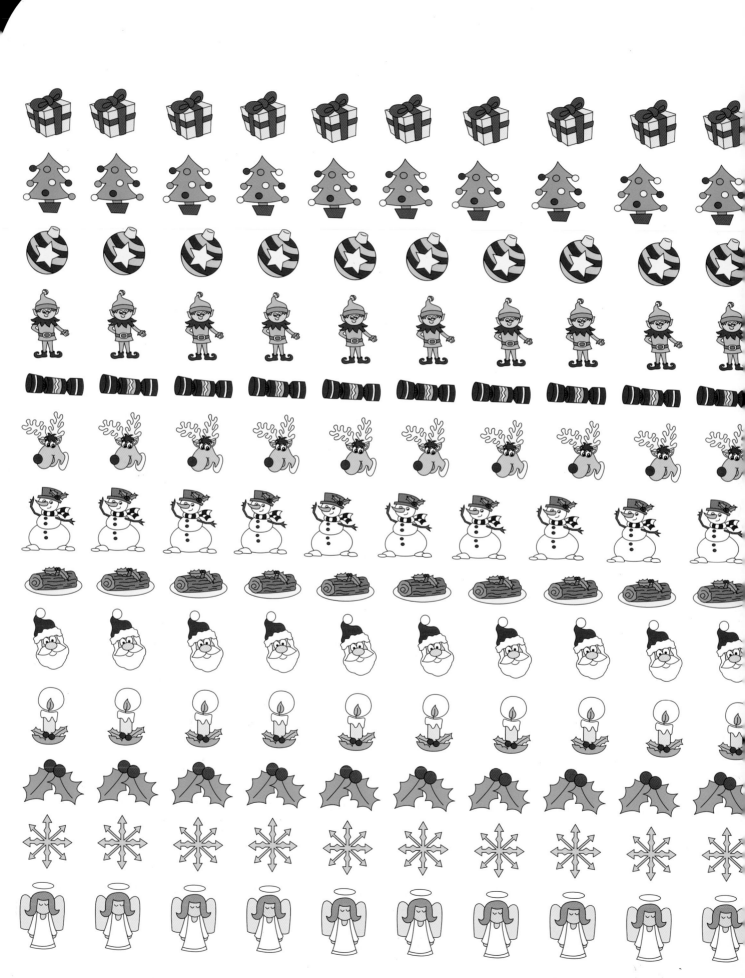

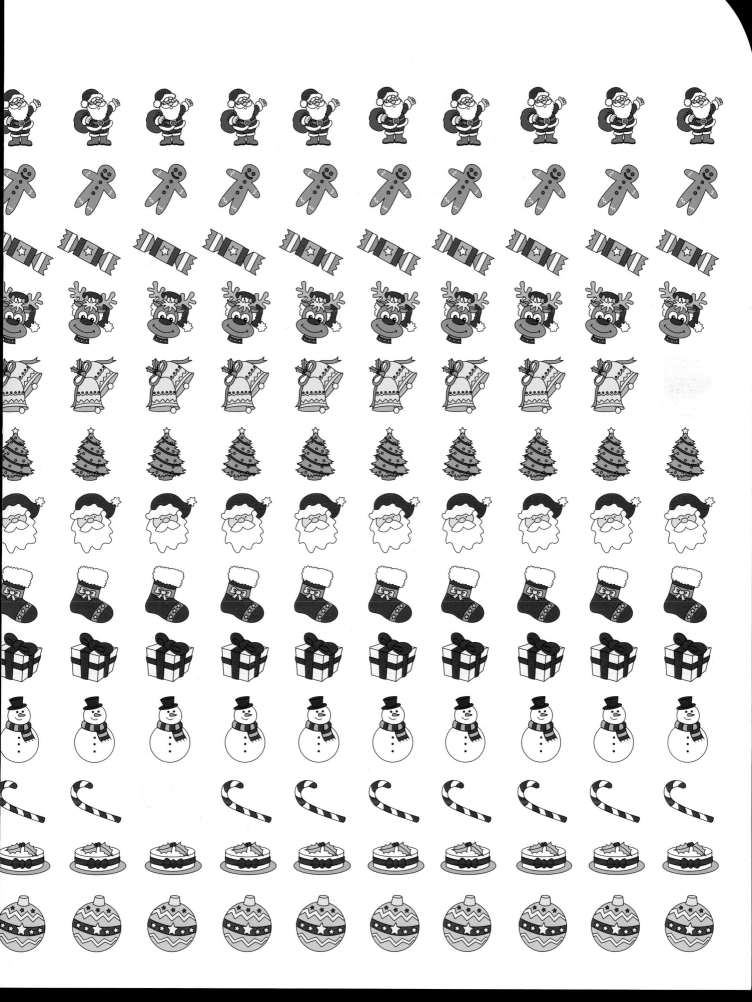

What is this snowman called? Cross out the letters that appear twice and the leftover letters will spell his name.

L	D	A	D
F	R	Z	A
L	H	O	H
B	M	C	Z
M	S	C	T
B	E	Y	E

What's going on top of the tree? Join the dots to find out, and then colour the whole picture.

Only two of these robins are exactly the same.
Can you see which ones?

It's Christmas Eve and the stockings are in place.
Colour this cosy scene.

Untangle the ribbons to find out which cheeky kitten is playing with each present.

Colour in the Christmas scene.

ANSWERS

1.

6.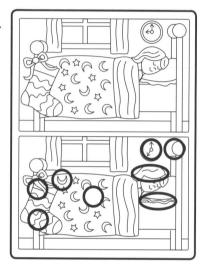

5.
1 =

2 =

3 =

4 =

9. FROSTY

11. D and E

13. A = 2
B = 3
C = 1